EVERYTHING I WRITE IS ABOUT YOU.

James McInerney

Also by James McInerney:

In Between the Lines.

Bloom.

Red.

The Pieces that Collide.

'EVERYTHING I WRITE IS ABOUT YOU'

THE WORDS I WROTE …THAT SPOKE OF HAPPINESS

IF YOU LOVE ME, BE PATIENT.
WITH MY WINGS, I FLY.
MY HEAVEN EXISTS IN YOU.
THE IDEA OF LOVING YOU.
WE ARE THE REAL STARS.
MEMORIES.
WHAT WE HAVE, WE WILL ALWAYS HAVE.
EMBRACE THE THINGS THAT SCARE YOU.
WALK ME THROUGH YOUR FIELDS OF HOPE.
YOU ARE MY CENTRE.
ONE DAY.
I DO NOT NEED A REASON.
A HOME FOR MY HEART.
RED LIGHT.
A FOG THAT CANNOT SETTLE.
GIVE ME ALL OF YOU.
I SURRENDER WITHOUT REGRET.
ETERNALLY YOURS.
WINTER.

'EVERYTHING I WRITE IS ABOUT YOU'

GOODBYE.
I MADE A PROMISE TO MY HEART.
I AM NO LONGER HELD BY YOU.
DEMONS.
DARKNESS.
WISH.
I AM DRAWN TO THE SEA.
I HAVE NOTEBOOKS FILLED WITH POETRY.
HURRICANE.
YOU HAVE CHANGED ME.
I DO NOT FEAR THE FALL.
DO NOT PROMISE ME THE STARS.
MY HEART.
YOU WILL NEVER BE MINE.
IT IS EASY TO THINK OF YOU AS THOUGH
YOU ARE MINE.
MY FALSE HOPE.
PARADISE.
I HAVE TRIED TO LOVE YOU LESS.
WE ARE TRAGICALLY INTERWOVEN.
WORDS.
I STOOD STILL TODAY.
OUR FINAL GOODBYE.
YOU LEFT ME.
FALLEN ANGEL.
I NO LONGER FEEL.
TIME.

'EVERYTHING I WRITE IS ABOUT YOU'

THE WORDS I WROTE ... TO AID MY RECOVERY

MAGIC.
MASTERPIECE.
WASTED ENERGY.
BE BRAVE.
COUNTERBALANCE.
STAND YOUR GROUND, OWN YOUR SPACE.
EMPTY HOUSES.
THE BEST KIND OF BEAUTIFUL.
FOOL'S GOLD.
NEW SHOES, NEW YOU!
SCARS.
STRENGTH.
A FEAST.
YOU DO NOT NEED TO CHANGE.
FIND YOUR MUSIC.
I WILL NOT RUN FROM YOU.
GRIEF AND LOSS.
CRASH AND BURN.
SUPERPOWER.
RECLAMATION DAY.
KNOW YOUR WORTH!
BLOOD IS BLOOD.
YOU.
CHANGE.
ASTRONAUT.
YOU ARE THE LIGHT.
FIND YOUR VOICE, CHANGE THE WORLD.

"You will never be able to fly if you remain tied to the things that keep you grounded."

- James McInerney

A massive thanks to the following people that have supported me via my Patreon account during the writing of this book. Your support means so much to me.

Patrons:

- Sally Anne Beere
- Sarah Elliott

https://www.patreon.com/jamesmcinerney

I cannot believe that I am on book five already! This book is slightly different from my previous books. For book number five, I wanted it to be more of a journey for the reader. As I was writing, in my head, I thought about relationships – the highs and the lows. Love is a minefield; it is a boat that has set sail on uncharted waters. It can be the best of times and the worst of times. Either way, relationships teach us things that we need to learn so that we can grow. This book reflects that. I hope you enjoy it. When it comes to love, always remember that you have a choice.

Speak soon,

James

THE
WORDS I
WROTE...
THAT
SPOKE OF
HOPE AND
HAPPINESS.

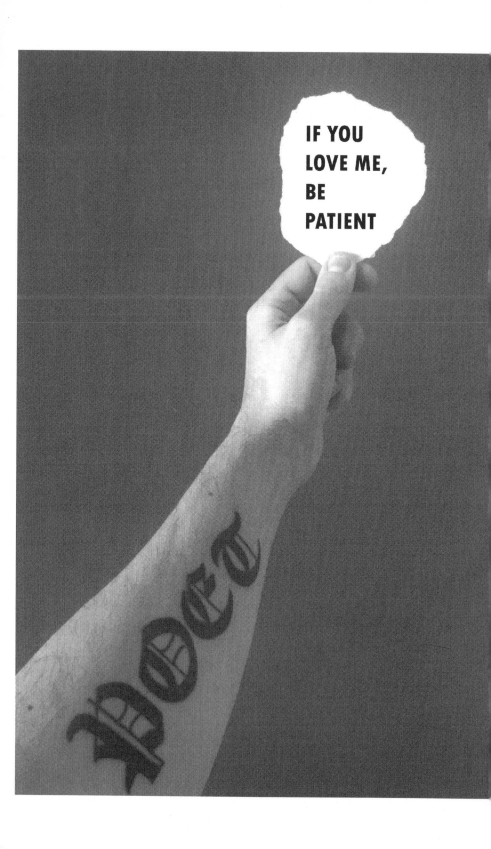

When it comes to my heart, you will never understand me if you cannot be patient. There will be times when I am silent, do not mistake my silence for weakness or neglect. When I feel things, I feel them deeply, my emotions often hold me hostage and render me immobile. Do not try to save me – I do not need saving, I need time and space so that I can process every impossible thought and balance it with a sense of reason. Only then will I feel comfortable in my own skin and you will get the version of me you rightly deserve.

James McInerney

I've always felt the
urge within me to fly.
Although life has my
heart grounded, it's
always at home in
your sky. It is the love
you have for me that
gives me my wings
and with my wings,
I fly.

James McInerney

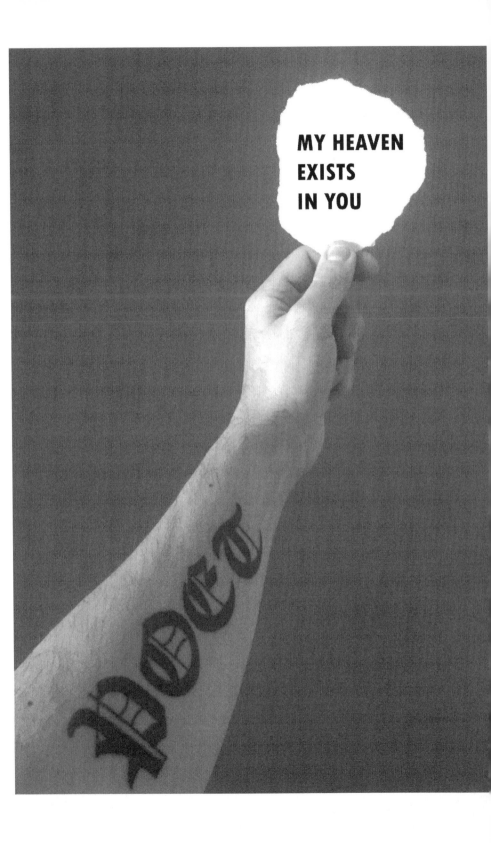

If you and I are to truly fall in the way we are supposed to fall, a promise of forever must firstly be made to the sky so that it can relieve us of our wings to aid the descent. Although I am fond of flying, I would willingly sacrifice my ability to visit a world that heaven overspills onto in exchange for a lifetime of existing in your presence.
I would have no need to climb to the dizzy heights in search of angels - I would have you.

James McInerney

THE IDEA
OF
LOVING
YOU

The idea of loving
you always seems
real to me
especially when
the only 'real' I
currently have in
my life right now
feels fake.

James McInerney

I have no desire to gain
altitude just to escape my
current atmosphere. My body
has grown used to the air, the
way it floods my lungs and
allows me to breathe freely.
I do not care for space or do I
spend my time worshipping
the sun. I dare say that the sun
is envious of us all – it knows
the real stars are present here
on earth and even though we
are grounded, we still manage
to shine brighter.

James McInerney

We are each other's memories, experiences yet to be had. Right now the timing isn't right but it will be and I promise you, when it is, we will have the time of our lives.

James McInerney

If anyone ever asked, I wouldn't
know where to begin when it
comes to explaining us.
We never really had a proper
beginning. We were two lost
souls who found each other at
the right time, somewhere in the
middle. We have spent so long
treading water, playing catch up,
that my head and my heart are
exhausted from the confusion.
If I know one thing to be true,
although we don't have a
beginning, we will never have an
end – an end is final and there is
nothing final about us, there
never will be.

James McInerney

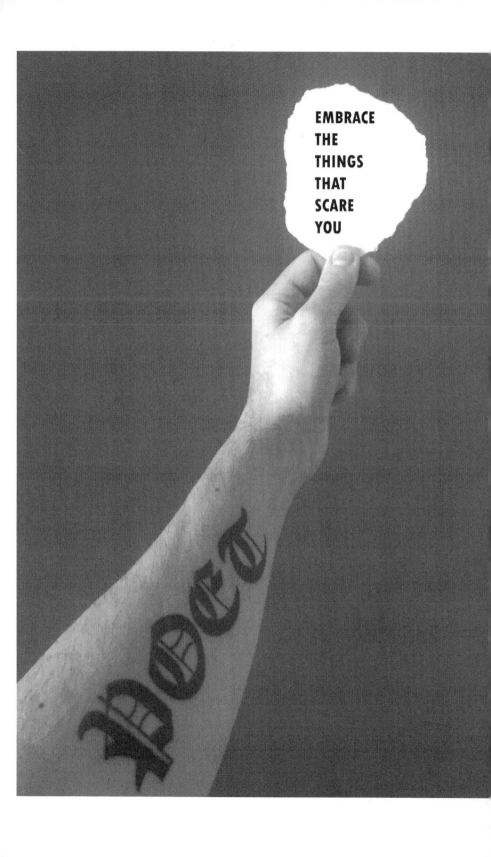

Embrace the things that scare you. You should never fear the unknown, even strangers can end up becoming the best of friends.

James McInerney

Walk me through your fields of hope, I know the love we'd share would be evergreen. My heart is lost, my spirit broke, all the hands I've held have led me astray and yet whilst I am in your presence, I am as present as the day.

James McInerney

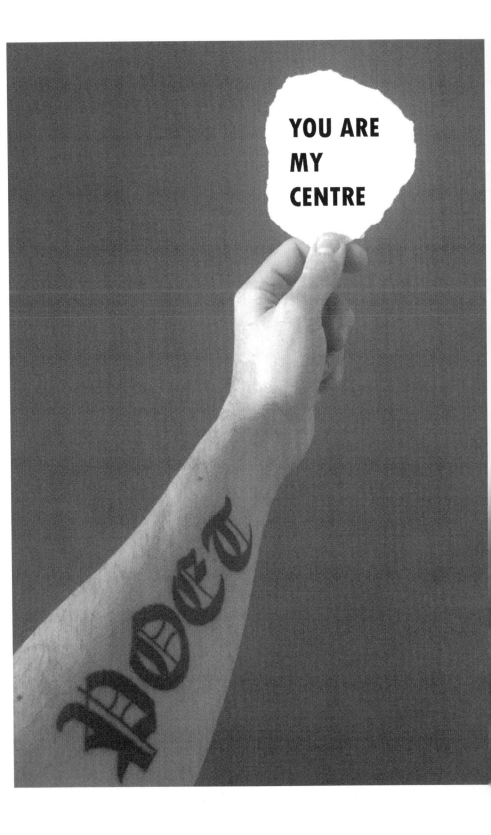

You are my centre.
I have been walking
towards you my entire
life, hopeful that one day
we will meet somewhere
in the middle. When it
comes to love, I have no
interest in triangles.
I see no value in moving
in never-ending circles
either, especially when
the centre is always the
heart of everything.

James McInerney

One day, you and I will fall apart in the most beautiful of ways and it won't matter to us where the pieces are scattered. Whoever finds what remains of our love and tries to make sense of us, could spend a lifetime and never even come close to understanding what we were and what we will always be.

James McInerney

I do not need a reason to love you less, I already have a lifetime of reasons to love you more.

James McInerney

When I first saw you,
I knew instantly that I
wouldn't have to
continue my search
to find a home for my
heart. You are the
walls, the beams, the
roof above my head
that sits proud and
strong.

James McInerney

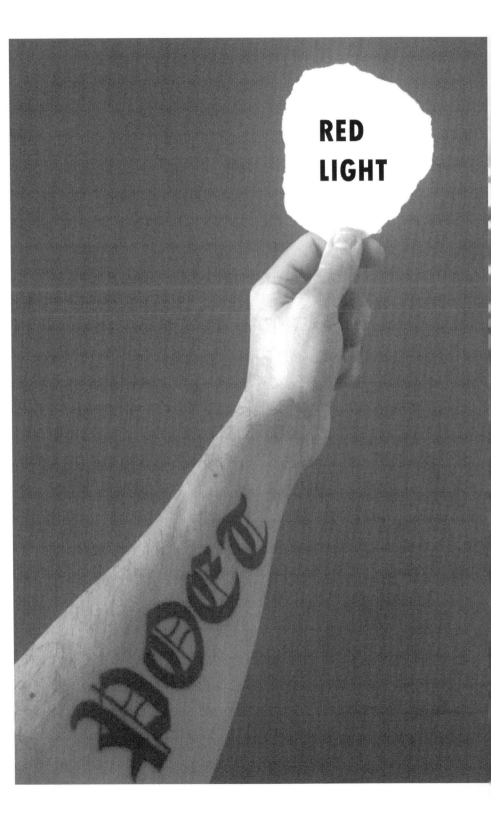

It wasn't until I got caught up in the wreckage with you, our bodies intertwined, that I felt the urge within me to run every red light thereafter. For me, slowing down was never an option.
To be brought to a standstill knowing full well that the distance between us remained untravelled was enough to awaken my senses and turn my heart fearless. I do not care about consequence or the collision. All that matters is that when it happens, it happens with you.

James McInerney

Whilst in your
presence, I am
weightless.
My body floats as
though you were a
sea of tranquillity
and the heaviness of
time,
a fog,
that cannot settle.

James McInerney

Give me everything, all
of you, I promise I'll
give you so much more
in return. You've spent
so long giving your
heart to the wrong
kind of fires that come
disguised as love, it's
no wonder you keep
getting burnt.

James McInerney

I surrender without regret; you disarm me like no other could. You are the sunrise that halts my sleep. Whenever I am stood before you, I always belong to a world that I have no desire to leave.

James McInerney

ETERNALLY
YOURS

I will love you
until I am no
more, and yet,
even then, you
will become the
song that plays
on repeat in my
mind.

James McInerney

WINTER

All the trees now sit, Winter bare,
their branches gathered
to survive the frost.
No leaves remain, the sun adrift,
bodies stolen without remorse.
The sky, the clouds, a heavy weight,
born to break upon command,
angels hurry toward the light,
braving each and every darkened void.
And yet I move, my spirit strong,
your music still ringing within my ears,
to dance is to live,
when the day seems bleak,
halting the cold so it cannot settle
- if permitted, settle it would.
In your absence,
I dance and think of you and me,
I dance whenever the day seems lost,
even the coldness of Winter
could never steal your warmth,
- it lives forever,
within my heart.

James McInerney

THE WORDS
I WROTE…
TO MAKE
SENSE OF
MY
SUFFERING.

You always seem to say
goodbye as though it's
easy for you.
The irony is that there
is nothing good about
goodbyes. They are a
lonely room filled with
never ending silence,
where all the broken
hearts wait in their own
personal hell.

James McInerney

I promised my heart
that I wouldn't dream
of you anymore
because it hurts way
too much and yet I
often find myself stood
alone, beneath the
night sky, assigning
your name to each and
every star that shines.

James McInerney

I am no longer held by you in
the way that I need to be held
so that my heart can feel
moved. The layers of warmth,
that were once bone deep,
bleed from my skin through
the cracks that refuse to close.
Where there was once light,
I am now exposed to the
ever-changing textures of
darkness. My focus is gone as
I am stood at the edge of
everything. I am a whisper
amongst the silence, an echo
without its sound.

James McInerney

DEMONS

You can't run
from your
demons

.

.

.

they follow.

James McInerney

I drank your darkness like a
thirsty soul, looking for love
in all the wrong places.
I mistook your varied
shades of grey for beautiful
colours and I painted them
proudly on my banner of
hope, only to realise that I
wasn't part of the parade.
As my hunger for you
lessened, I found myself
belonging to a different kind
of procession …
a funeral procession …
mine.

James McInerney

Always be careful
what you wish for,
even the best kind
of wish can bring
about the worst
kind of heartache,
especially when
love is involved.

James McInerney

I am drawn to the sea and
in turn, the sea, me.
Its salty tide, my salty
tears. The heights and
depths at which I roam
are affectionately mirrored
with every ebb and flow.
We dance a dance and
that dance is true.
We rise, we fall, we rage,
we bleed and yet to the
sea I am drawn and in
turn, the sea, me.

James McInerney

I started writing down all the
words we used to share the
moment you stopped saying
them. My heart spent so long
being told it was loved, it was
easier to continue living a lie
than accept the truth that I was
never going to hear those
words from you again.
I now have notebooks filled
with poetry. A place I thought
would hide me, but you are
everywhere, you were
everything to me.

James McInerney

HURRICANE

You were my hurricane.

I was uprooted,

sucked in,

my heart spun,

only to be left wild,

disorientated

and

alone.

James McInerney

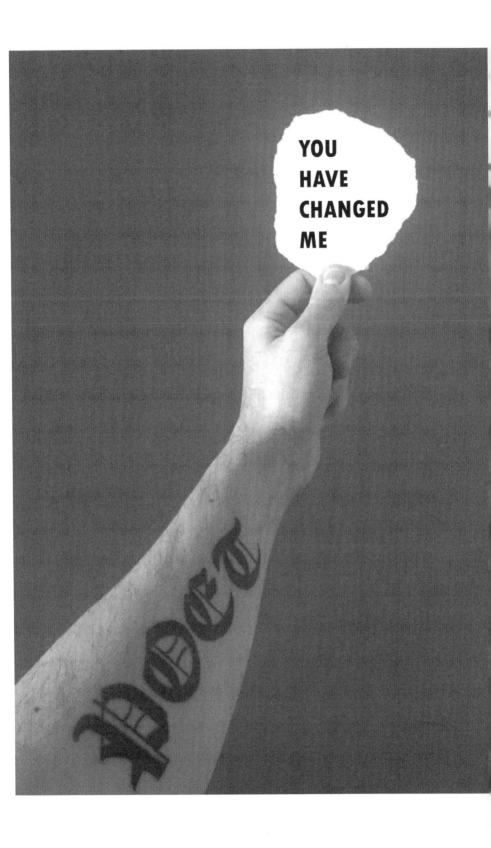

You have changed me,
I'm not the person I once
was. Before I met you, I
never realised how much
one person could light
up an entire room just by
being in it. Now that
you've gone, I find myself
drawn to the darkness,
craving the light, in the
hope you'll return.

James McInerney

I do not fear the fall,
gravity always wins,
it's never a choice.
What I fear is falling
alone, without you,
knowing that the
impact will shatter my
bones and you won't
be around to help put
my broken pieces back
together.

James McInerney

I believed you when you told
me that the air was breathable.
I burnt the supporting beams,
knowing my walls would fall
because you convinced me that
I didn't need to live with the
comfort of a roof above my
head if I had you.
You promised me that the stars
would be enough and yet, when
the sky opened up and your
eyes saw an entire universe of
opportunity, your gaze was set
on a destination that took you
as far from us as you could
possibly be.

James McInerney

MY
HEART

My heart always
aches for reasons
that it shouldn't,
in ways that it
shouldn't,
for people that
don't deserve the
love I always
willingly give.

James McInerney

You are
the water,
the river,
a sea of forever
that will never
be mine.

James McInerney

It is easy to think of you as though you are mine. You are the answer to all my questions and yet you are not mine, in the same way that I am not yours. A question that I ask myself on a daily basis, one which never seems to have an answer.

James McInerney

I now
understand
what you
were...
my
false
hope.

James McInerney

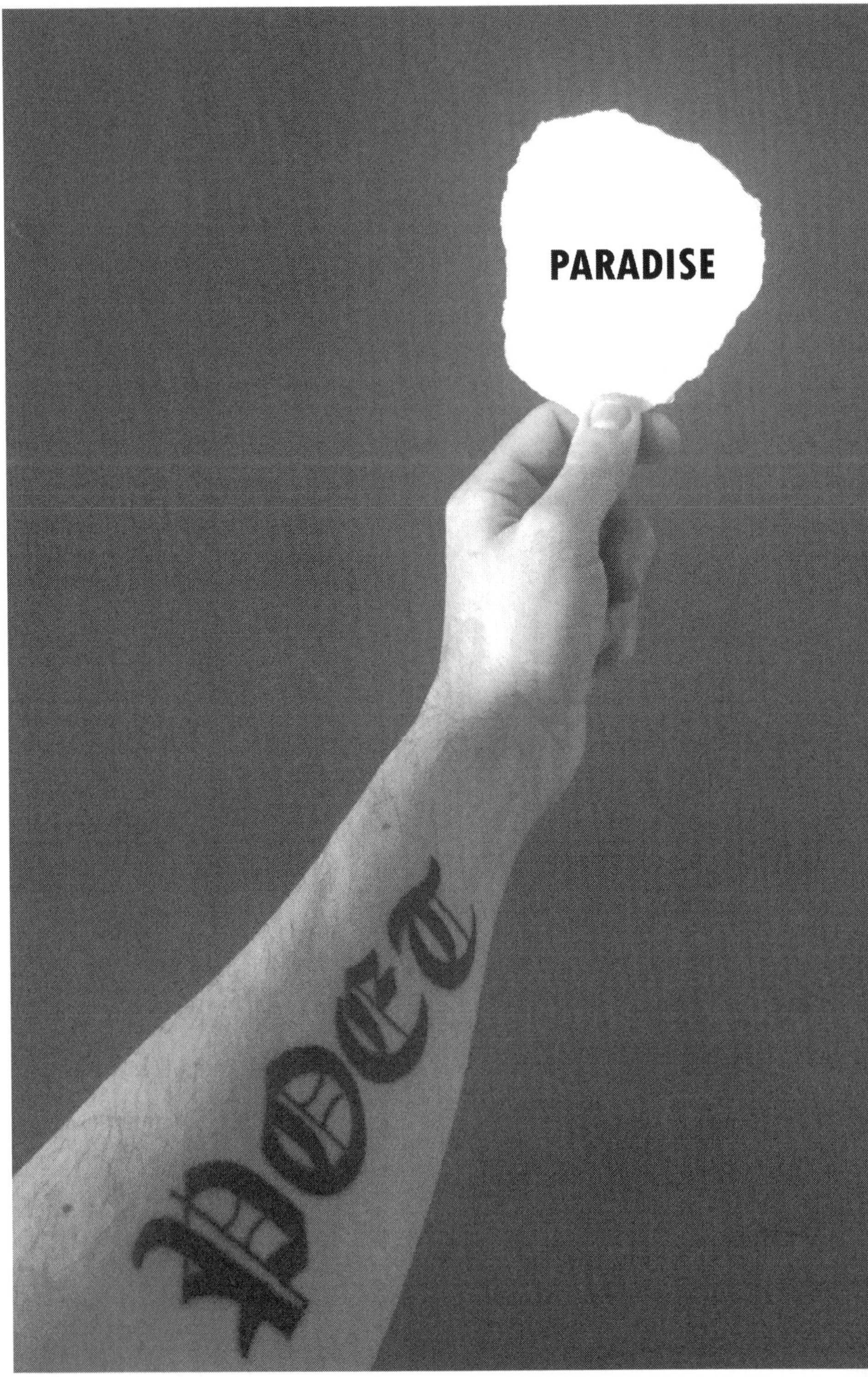
PARADISE

You never truly understood me, not in the way I wanted you to. Your eyes always saw love as though it were a glorious day and the second the storms took hold; the sails were raised, and you were off in search of paradise.

James McInerney

I have tried to love you less but, in my attempts to do so, I found that I ended up loving you even more.

James McInerney

You always have the
ability to open old
wounds, even when we
don't speak. We remain
tangled; my heart is drawn
to you for reasons that
escape me and yet I
cannot escape you.
I will never be free.
My broken pieces are
being held together by
the constant pull of your
invisible thread.

James McInerney

If I can't physically be with you then hopefully my words can because they are always about you, even the ones that were hard to write.

James McInerney

I stood still today,
when the whole
world demanded
that I move.
I had no words to
say and yet I was
expected to
speak.

James McInerney

Our final goodbye
should be so painful
that it should tear the
heavens apart so
there is nothing good
left to look forward to
in this world because
without you, I would
have nothing good left
in mine.

James McInerney

You didn't
just leave,
you left me
with feelings
for you that
will remain
forever.

James McInerney

The sound of your voice as it broke
without warning,
all the tears that betrayed you and
refused to hide.
The way that you fell to your knees
hoping someone would save you,
a fallen angel,
without reprieve,
caught in the tide.
Your body,
a flicker,
a flame,
now rests and yet it does so
without ease.
I occupy the same space that once
occupied you,
it holds me in such a way that I am
unable to leave.

James McInerney

At the centre of
me, everything
sits cold.
I no longer feel
and yet I have
never felt so
alone.

James McInerney

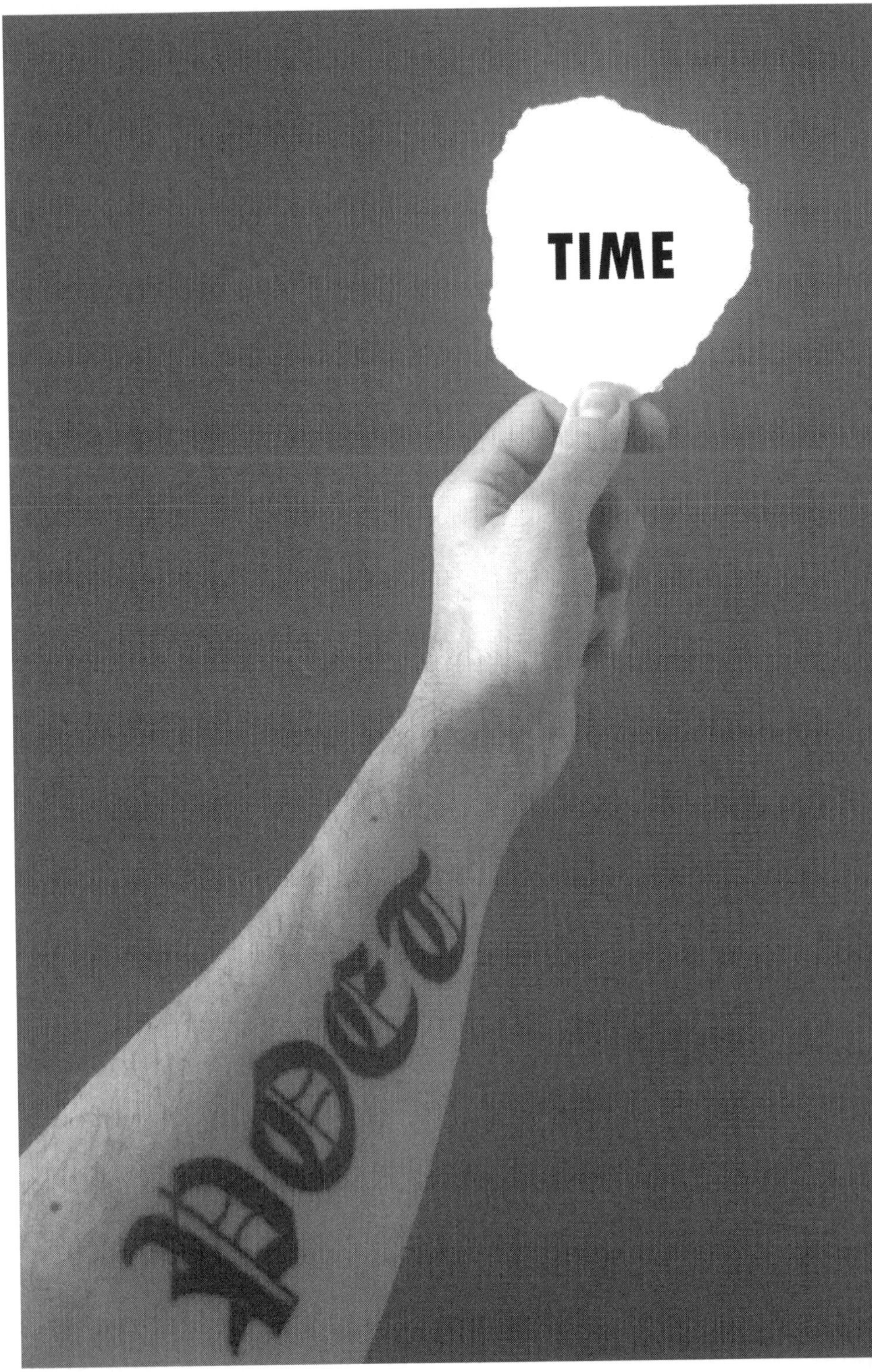
TIME

I no longer know what to do with the
empty spaces that remain, they exist in
the same way that I exist and yet I
barely exist at all. Time doesn't move
for me anymore. I see it. I feel it.
I hear it but I am no longer part of it.
We parted ways the day I held you
wanting nothing but time, to have to
watch time fade from you as though it
didn't matter as though you didn't
matter but you mattered to me.
You were all that mattered to me.
I remember holding you in my arms,
my whole world filled with time, living,
breathing, moving and yet you were
not. You were no longer you and I was
no longer me and, in that moment, I
decided I no longer cared for time if
you were no longer part of it.

James McInerney

THE
WORDS I
WROTE...
TO AID MY
RECOVERY.

MAGIC

I now realise that I never needed to be guided by your hand as though I didn't know my own mind. I spent a lifetime trapped inside a world created by you, the exit always hidden through misdirection and a series of cheap parlour tricks, cleverly disguised as love to keep me contained. I foolishly believed that you were the 'one' and all I needed to do was to walk your path and there would be an abundance of nourishment to keep me sustained. I now know it was a lie, an illusion — you are a master of your craft. The flowers always bloomed in accordance to the season, the sun knew its place as did the stars and the moon and in turn I knew my place too. I smiled. I obeyed. I bit my tongue. Whilst others marvelled at your sleight of hand, I had your well-rehearsed act memorised. What you didn't notice, as the crowds were up on their feet applauding you, is that I would stay sat in my seat. A hidden thorn amongst your bed of roses. A succulent.

Slowly draining your admirers, knowing that they would turn on you when you could no longer provide and grow to despise you as much as I did and still do now. After learning all your tricks, it would have been easy for me to disappear, but I chose to stay. I found the courage within myself to set the white rabbit free so you could no longer have that level of control over anyone or anything. In your final performance as I stood clapping, a beacon of light, a voice amongst the silence, your sea of worshippers finally saw you for what you really were – fake magic. A magician without a rabbit. The real magic, the one thing that you didn't see coming, was me. I learnt that you must make friends with your demons – they teach you things about yourself that you need to learn in order to grow as a person. Without realising, you taught me everything I needed to know and with that knowledge, by my hand, in the end, it was me who made you disappear.

James McInerney

You must never fear your level of
darkness as though it's something
that defines you as a person.
If you are to grow, it's important that
you acknowledge and embrace your
sharp edges too. What you see in
you as 'flaws' and 'imperfections', to
the trained eye, are unplanned brush
strokes, where the creator got
caught up in the moment because
the moment made them feel alive.
When people fall in love, they are
captivated by the details.
Your details are your broken pieces.
You were once whole, and life broke
you and yet here you are, a living,
breathing, masterpiece, a work of art.

James McInerney

You can't lose
something that wasn't
yours to begin with,
in the same way that
there is no point
searching the sky for
stars after the sun
has risen – you won't
find what you are
looking for.

James McInerney

It takes real courage to continue to live in a house and call it a home, knowing full well it contains rooms that hold memories that cause you pain. Locked doors tend to highlight the things they are designed to hide and, in the process, further add to the feeling of isolation. You will never heal if you refuse to acknowledge your demons – they will remind you of their presence and there will be no escape from the daily torment. Be brave. Open every door. Face what you fear, head on. Ghosts from your past have no place in your future.

James McInerney

COUNTER
BALANCE

Do not underestimate the level of power that I possess. I will not fall in the way you expect me to, I will not conform just to suit your ever-changing needs. My legs will not buckle under your pressure as though weak. When we collide, which of course we will, the heavy weight that you constantly placed upon my shoulders will become the counterbalance that will keep my spine rooted to the earth so that I remain nourished. It will allow me to stand tall, it will support me as I grow in confidence. You will see me flourish before your eyes, it will become a constant reminder of what you lost. I will breathe you in, consuming all the air that surrounds me so that when I breathe out, you will finally be gone from my life forever.

James McInerney

You do not need to change who you are just to fit the mould, cast by a broken society. Stick to your values, make choices that offer long-term fulfilment instead of short-term solutions that lead nowhere. There is no turning back when you have sold your soul and the veil drops and you see the mirage for what it truly is – an empty highway, sign posted with places that you will never reach.

You are worth more than that.

Stand your ground.

Own your space.

James McInerney

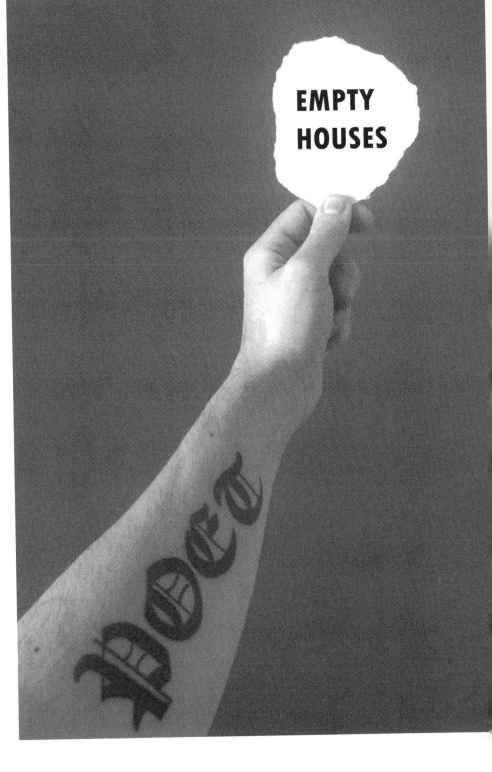

The inner power you possess is god given. It is unique in the same way that you are and cannot be duplicated as though interchangeable.
Believe me when I tell you that you are a beautiful anomaly.
You are not, or will you ever be, standard or normal. You are a wonder, a miracle. You do not have to satisfy the needs of others with answers to questions that attempt to define you as a person, just so they can sleep better at night.
I say, deny them their sleep, leave them to live their empty lives in their empty houses with their insecurities and then sit back and watch how they boast, despite it all, that they are truly living.

James McInerney

THE BEST
KIND
OF
BEAUTIFUL

Your poetry is going
to be raw and
emotional and it
might not flow
perfectly but it's
you.
You spilled your
heart out on the
page and that's the
best kind of
beautiful there is.

James McInerney

FOOL'S
GOLD

I know you are suffering right now but please know that the pain you are currently feeling has not gone unnoticed.
It fills the loudest of rooms and silences the voices of those that speak ill of you. Even at your weakest, believe me when I say that you are bigger, better and stronger than the fools that seek gold and yet just by being in your presence, do not realise the level of wealth they possess.

James McInerney

Today is the day that your eyes will be
opened to a new way of living, however,
your approach must be completely
different.

You can't walk a new path in old shoes,
your feet will remain as comfortable as
they once did, the tread will be just as
worn, and you will end up slipping into
old habits and it is the old habits that are
sometimes the hardest to shake.

Buy new shoes, pricey ones, with good
soles. You have a lot of walking ahead of
you, especially if you are looking to
distance yourself from the all-seeing eyes
that only see what they want to see.

You don't need them, in fact, you don't
need anyone. You are stronger than you
realise.

I know it might seem impossible; those
first initial steps will be the hardest.

But as one bad day ends, a new one, full
of promise always begins. I promise you,
as your eyes open and the sun rises to
mark the start of a new day, you'll find
yourself breathing cleaner air and
wearing shoes that you'll always cherish
because they took you where you needed
to be - a better place, a better you.

James McInerney

SCARS

Her scars are not imperfections. They are her daily reminder that the struggle is real, as is her desire to overcome it.

James McInerney

It took me time to realise my own
strength, to realise that you were just
drip-feeding me to keep me hungry and
manageable. As your self-confidence
grew, mine did too. I did not feed from
you to satisfy my hunger. I fed from you
because you foolishly gave thinking I
needed to be fed, unaware that I had no
appetite whilst in your presence.
All the time I was feeding, I was growing,
I was learning how to survive on the
scraps you deemed adequate.
In my mind, they became a feast and that
feast sustained me. What you saw as
weakness, became my strength and I
realised that I no longer needed to be
nourished by you in order to survive.
In fact, I realised that I no longer needed
you at all.

James McInerney

A
FEAST

The only way that your heart
will triumph at the hands of
love is if those hands are your
own. When we embrace and
acknowledge that it is our
divine right to be loved and
that it is god given, the shrine
that is our body will become
the altar at which we worship,
without fear, every single day.
When we understand the true
calling of our heart, only then
will we allow those who are
worthy enough to feast, the
freedom of our inner sanctum,
knowing full well that in turn
they shall become a feast too.

James McInerney

Trust me when I tell you that you are worthy of so much more. The reason you are currently feeling unnoticed and unloved is down to failings beyond your control. Do not put yourself through torture just because commitment is an impossible thought for the kind of people who are afraid to be real about how they truly feel. They need to change, you don't.

James McInerney

In a moment of clarity, she
found herself belonging to the
words of a song, one that had
always been written for her.
She had somehow allowed
herself to be convinced by the
world that the lyrics had no
purpose or value and yet as
she heard every uplifting verse,
she regained what she had
once lost:
her rhythm,
her music,
herself.

James McInerney

I will not run from you; my heart
isn't yours in the way it once was.
I shall live my life in plain sight,
no longer hidden by your desire
to keep me forbidden.
I will breathe. I'll be fire. I will
have the freedom I didn't, when I
was with you. I will dance to the
music you made me forget.
I will not tire, I will not rest.
There will no longer be a heavy
ache that I carry within my chest.
Every footstep, every moment will
be brand new. You will see, you
will know, how effortlessly I can
move now that I have shed the
layer of skin that I grew when I
was with you.

James McInerney

GRIEF
AND
LOSS

When it comes to grief
and loss, sometimes
you must embrace the
storm to survive the
chaos. Those that run
will spend a lifetime
running at speeds
fuelled by fear and
regret, constant
companions that never
truly leave regardless of
the distance travelled.

James McInerney

When you no longer recognise yourself in a situation that no longer recognises you, it's time to walk away and remove the fuel from the fire that is only there to convince you that it's you who needs to change. You don't. You can't keep feeding something that refuses to grow, it is wasted energy. We all have our breaking point; it is there for a reason but it should never be seen as a weakness if we crash and burn. It takes real courage to let go of the steering wheel and face the collision head on knowing it is going to hurt like hell. Yes, you will ache in places that were once filled with love but where there is pain there is also beauty and I promise you that you will emerge from the wreckage a better person.
All the things you leave behind will have mattered because they will have taught you what really matters...you.

James McInerney

In the end it was her
brokenness that
became her
superpower.
The moment she
realised that her
vulnerability was
also her strength,
she saved herself
instead.

James McInerney

There will be days where you will feel perfectly in tune with your body, cherish those moments. When we completely fall out of touch with our inner self, the divide becomes apparent to those who know us well and in the process, we end up isolating ourselves from the people that matter the most. It is important to celebrate 'oneness', that rare moment when our opposing thoughts and feelings find a common ground. All those tight bends, those dangerous corners, suddenly become an open road. You will find yourself cruising, soft top down, the wind in your hair, without a care in the world. It is important that you reclaim the parts of yourself that were always yours - that level of validation will be like a fuse being lit. It will be like a pin, pulled from its grenade. Of course there will be fire, the sky will inevitably fall but the impact will be the catalyst that will wake you from your sleep and open your eyes to a life filled with love and laughter and days that you will never want to end.

James McInerney

If people cannot see
your worth, they are
not worthy of your
precious time and are
blind to the abundance
of riches that you
possess. It is only
when we truly value
those around us that
we reap the rewards.

James McInerney

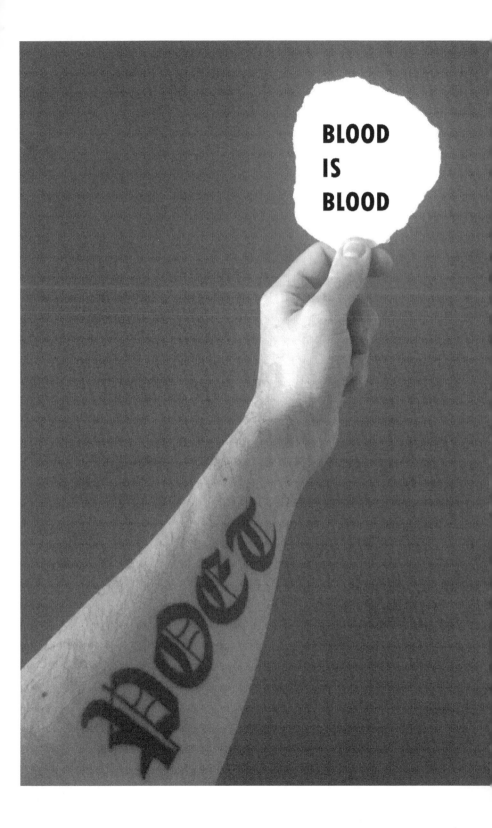

When the moment gets tough and
the heaviness refuses to leave,
no one has the right to tell you how
you are supposed to feel.
Blood is blood. All of us bleed.
Our hearts may break in similar
ways, but they heal at different
speeds. For some, it's a graze, an
insignificant bruise, a room where
the exits are clearly defined and yet
there are others who struggle, their
wounds as deep as the daily
thoughts that plague their mind.
Do not be silenced by people that
do not understand your level of pain.
Be vocal. Shout and scream if you
have to. When we acknowledge the
darkness, it no longer remains
hidden from the light and only then
can the healing process begin.

James McInerney

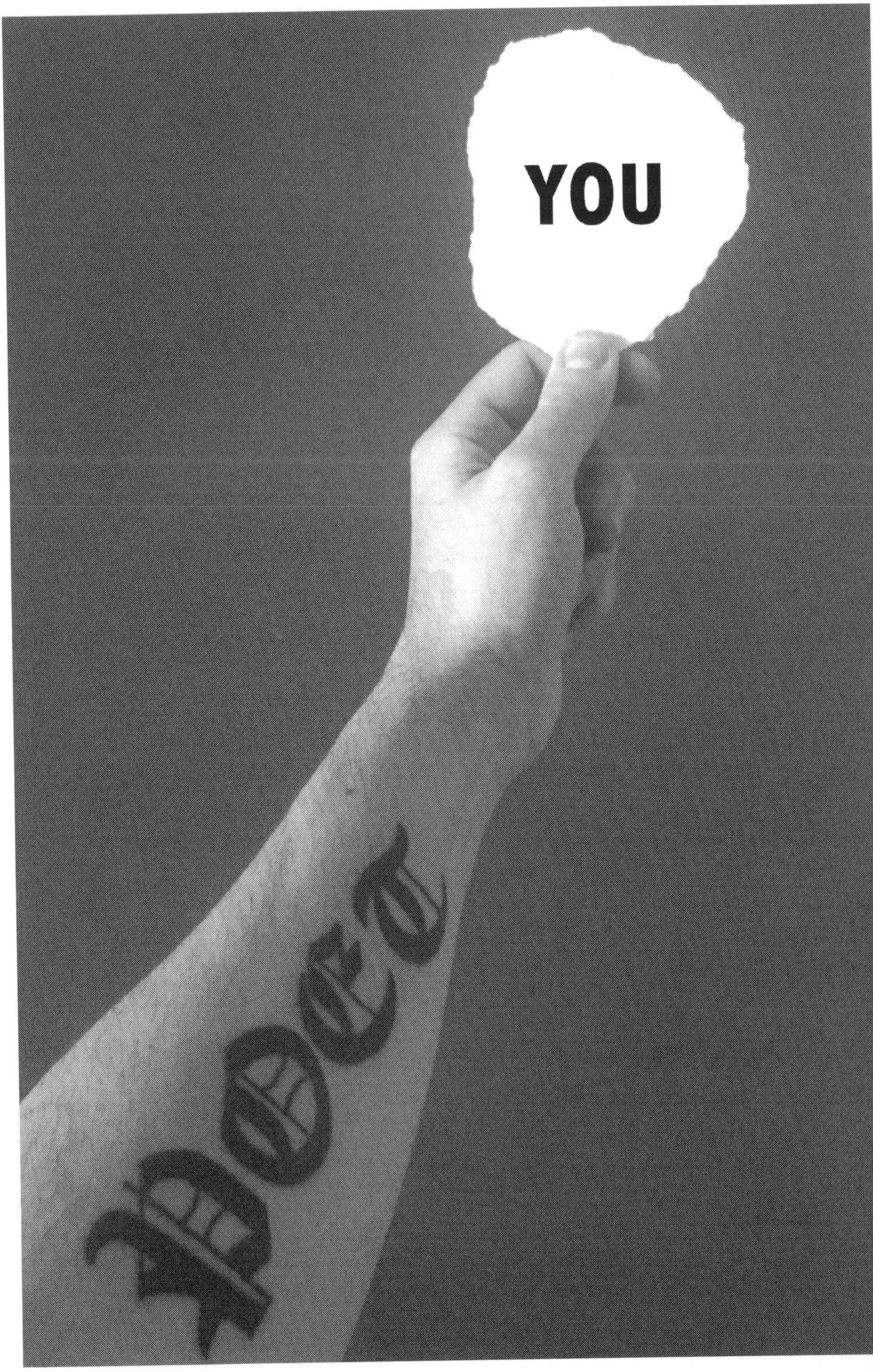
YOU

I will not burn;
I will learn from
my mistakes.
I might be a
river of tears but
all rivers
eventually flow
to the sea - you.

James McInerney

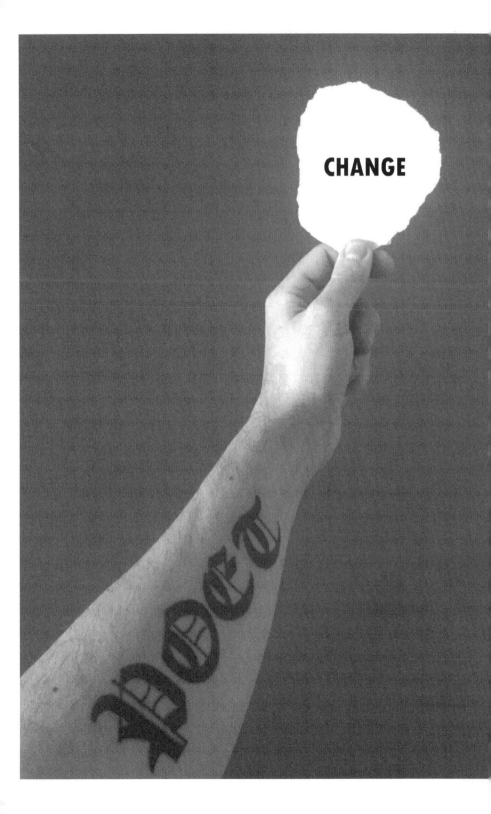

CHANGE

The kind of people that are stood before the storm, understand the need for change, quicker than those that hide from it. It's not your responsibility to carry the weight of the world on your shoulders – all you are doing is lightening the load on a system that is already flawed and needs to break. If you want change, the kind that makes waves, you can't pick a fight with the sea - you'll never win, its tides are too strong.
Real change begins in the rivers, in the streams, amongst the overlooked and the underappreciated but you must not allow your body to become a refuge for all the broken souls. Their sharp edges will wound you and that wound will rot. Seek them out, embrace them, educate them, but do not offer them sanctuary from the storm - a storm happens for a reason, it brings about change.

James McInerney

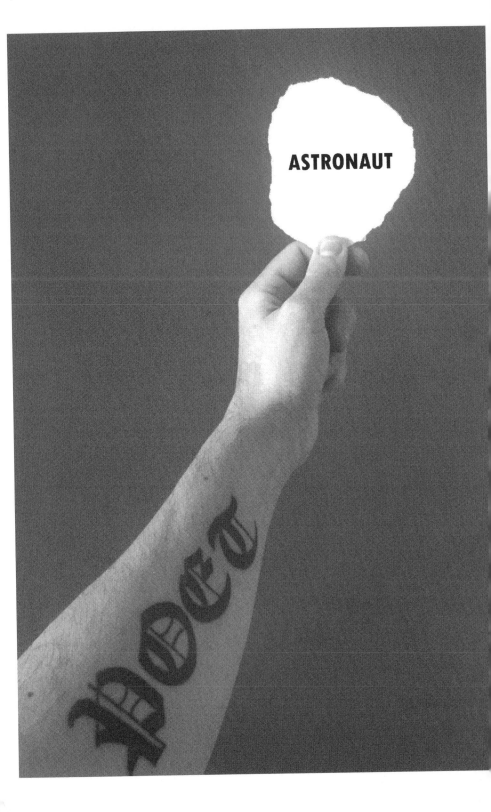

ASTRONAUT

I used to be your everything,
your entire universe and yet
you need space?
Astronauts go to space, they
explore other planets in search
of life. My life is happening
right now on this planet.
If you can't see that, if you
can't see me, if loving me is
alien to you, then I will gladly
be there on the day of your
launch just to make sure you
exit my atmosphere and I no
longer have to breathe you in.

James McInerney

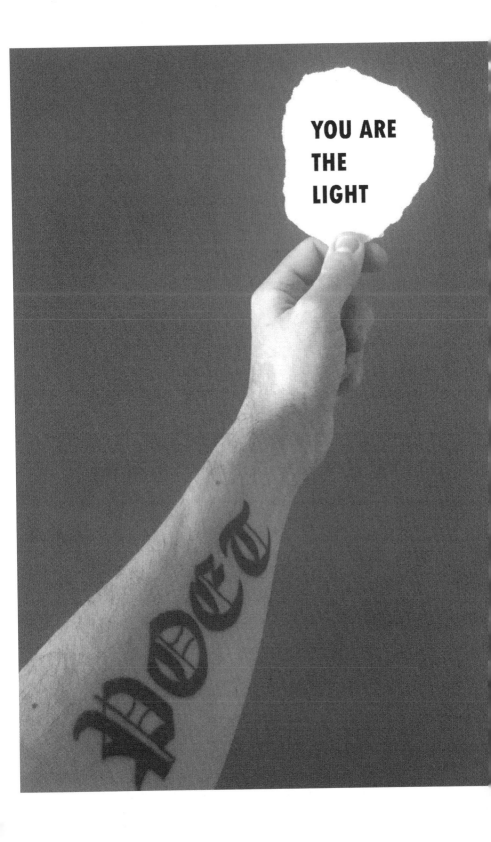

You are the light;
you have no
reason to be
afraid of the dark.
The way you
shine, the
shadows fear you
more.

James McInerney

Communication is important, it is the key that unlocks the door to a world full of change. Life doesn't have to be as complicated as we make it. The more we talk to each other, the moment we take that leap of faith and express how we are truly feeling instead of bottling it all up, the quicker we will realise that we are the answer to each other's questions. Sometimes change can come about from something as simple as "hello" or "how are you feeling today?". It is easy to lose sight of what's important, we are all different. Individuality should be celebrated. We all think, we all feel, we are all capable of love and hate in equal amounts, but we also have the ability to choose. It is in all our interests to make that choice to help, support and to talk to each other. If we have a better understanding of each other, there will be less confusion. If there is less confusion, there is more room for change, more room for peace, more room for us all to live in the way we are supposed to be living – together.

James McInerney

James grew up in an area in Northampton aptly named 'Poets Corner', unbeknownst that poetry was to become a huge part of his life.
Having no prior interest in the subject matter in his younger years, James discovered the wonders of writing in his twenties.
Mixing his own thoughts and emotions with classical and instrumental film scores, he realised for the first time in his life that there was more to writing than met the eye.
With no real influences or coming from a writing background, James' enthusiasm grew and grew, and it was full steam ahead – with no turning back!
Not content with writing words for his own amusement, he continued to test the boundaries - to great effect.
Using his new-found love for writing and his in-depth knowledge of social networking sites, his resourcefulness resulted in success.
As his work is becoming more popular, his numbers are growing on his social networking sites; James has 33,000 followers on Instagram and 11,000 on Twitter.
Attracting a lot of attention over the years, James and his works have covered a wide range of different media platforms.
With his works, he has been featured in various UK and International magazines and newspapers and has been featured on various radio stations in the UK and the Netherlands including the BBC (where he is a part of the newspaper review team).
His words have been adapted and performed by many musicians and vocalists, with many of them gaining a lot of airplay on multiple radio stations. His first book was also used in a sci-fi American TV show.
With various US/UK Actors and Actresses voicing his poetry, James is taking his words to a whole new level.
His books 'In between the Lines', 'Bloom', 'Red' and 'The Pieces that Collide' are currently available to buy via Amazon Worldwide and are also available to read for free in various Schools, Colleges, Universities and Libraries in the UK, Ireland and America.

Keep up to date with James and his latest works on any of the following sites:

Official Website: http://jamesmcinerney.wixsite.com/poetry

Email: jeeter77@gmail.com

Social sites

Facebook:

https://www.facebook.com/borntobeapoet

https://www.facebook.com/groups/JamesTMcInerney/

https://www.facebook.com/jamesmcinerneypoetry/

https://www.facebook.com/groups/thepoetryproject08/

Twitter: https://twitter.com/MillsMc07

Instagram: https://www.instagram.com/millsmc07/

Tumblr: https://www.tumblr.com/blog/jamesmcinerneyofficial

LinkedIn: https://www.linkedin.com/in/james-mcinerney-661561128/

Goodreads:
https://www.goodreads.com/author/show/4733780.James_McInerney

Pinterest: https://www.pinterest.co.uk/jeetmc07/

Mirakee: http://www.mirakee.com/jamesmcinerney

YouTube: http://www.youtube.com/user/millsmc1977

We Heart It: https://weheartit.com/millsmc07

WordPress: https://wordpress.com/view/borntobeapoet.wordpress.com

Lettrs: https://lettrs.com/jamesmcinerney

Patreon: https://www.patreon.com/jamesmcinerney

Snapchat: millsmc07

Vero: @millsmc07

Printed in Poland
by Amazon Fulfillment
Poland Sp. z o.o., Wrocław

54138729R00092